Thanks For Your
Thoughtfulness
Enjoy

Copyright © 2015 by Ann Chestnut

All rights reserved.
No part of this book may be used or reproduced in any manner without written permission except in the case of brief quotations in critical articles or reviews

Drawings by Ann Chestnut

Available from Amazon.com and other distributors.

ISBN-13: 978-0-578-16375-8

DEDICATION

This book is dedicated to all volunteers who selflessly give of their time toward benefitting others. I want to especially acknowledge those of the Allegan, Michigan area, including financial donors, without whom the following programs could not exist:

Congregational Kitchen Meals- Volunteers of this program prepare more than 900 homemade meals for public distribution every Thursday night. Donations are needed for the packaging supplies necessary to provide this service.

School Lunch Packs- A group of volunteers delivering over 300 weekend meals for Allegan Public School students each week. Donations are used to purchase milk and other items needed to provide nutritionally balanced meals.

Congregational Food Warehouse- Serving 28 pantries and community kitchens through the distribution of food and supplies generously donated by private corporations. Donations are needed for operational costs of the warehouse, such as rent, refrigeration equipment, and utilities.

By purchasing this book, you are supporting their efforts, as I will donate, at minimum, fifty-percent of book proceeds to these programs. Please join me by demonstrating your appreciation for the service, thoughtfulness, patience, and non-judgmental attitudes towards others volunteers provide.

Ann Chestnut
Allegan, Michigan
2015

Some people wonder if they should ask for help
Others wonder if they should ask to help

Some of the best memories made
Do not come with an "on/off" button
And go forever without recharging

<><><>

Peoples make for an interesting puzzle
All shapes---all sizes---all colors
When assembled together
A beautiful picture of life it makes

<><><>

Lingering Thoughts

If you had known me before—
    would you still want to know me today?
You have met me today—
    will you look forward to seeing me again?
You have felt my positive vibes—
    will they bring you back to renew?
You have seen my smile—
    on an ordinary day will it bring a smile to you?
You have heard my dreams—
    will they encourage you to wonder?
You have witnessed my imagination—
    will it inspire what hides in your mind?
You have shared my thoughtfulness—
    will you share yours with others?

The answers are, "Yes!"
Because these are your attributes that come to my mind—
    when I think of you

Happy Birthday

The reservation for you on my dance card has arrived
When I rock with you my heart comes alive
An easy rock back and forth seems to please
My arms wrapped around you like parenthesis
Dancing like this as though we are one
Nurtures a relationship never to be undone
Your own dance card for you awaits
It was given to you on your birth date
Prints on your certificate are ready for a future dance
I look forward to a reservation at every chance
Your dance is changing as you spend time on the floor
It is your breakdance moves that help you explore
No more just standing and holding on tight
Freedom of footprints will be moving tonight
Your dancing of patterns all over the floor
Applause from everyone demanding an encore
Feel the energy that flows from each event
Not better—not worse—just different
Everyone born has their own dance card to use
Dance alone or together it is your personal style to choose
To take part in life's dance
Never miss any chance

Baggage

Might not have wheels
so you lug it
The handle is gone
you wrap your arms around it
You continue to lug it
Might not be visible
Your body language shows you are still lugging it
Now you have to upgrade to a larger size
A little more bend in the body
but you still lug it

Enough is enough

Find a place to cast off your baggage
You have collected it all your life
You have lugged it all your life
When you get to the end
you cannot take it with you anyway

Life

Life is a team event
    Choose wisely

Life is a series of continuous events
    Volunteer your energy

Life is full of ideas that never take flight
    Celebrate them as experiences

Life is liberty in your personal space
    Know your boundaries

Life is a given for you
    So is it for me

Life is the pursuit of happiness
    Make it happen

Life is not full of entitlements
    but opportunities to bloom

Life is not instant gratification
    but needs time to simmer

Life is not about you
>   but what you secretly do for others

Be grateful for life, liberty and
>   the pursuit of happiness

Join the celebration when
>   you recognize the melody

Sing along
>   Life is a harmony

It

If you have It
    Appreciate It

If you are given It
    Teach with It

If you sense It
    Test It

If you had It
    Search for It

If you are looking for It
    Question who has It

If you flaunt It
    You only think you have It

If you want It
    Reach for It

If you recognize It
    You have shared It

Maturity?

Hair is receding
Mind is forgetting
Eyelids are drooping
Nose is running
Earlobes are elongating
Chin is doubling
Chest is sagging
Muffin top is expanding
Behind is tilting
Knees are creaking
Ankles are turning
Do not make it worst by having your mouth flapping
Be thankful it is just the change in the wrapper and
celebrate the fact that you are still breathing and
you have a heart that is still loving

Friendship

Forget not how and what I said
Remember there is some good in everything
Illuminate the days for others
Expect the best
Never doubt what our time together means
Delight in memories made
Share your visions with others
Help those who cannot speak for themselves
Illustrate what you desire from others
Pause— give thanks— for your relationships

Climb to the top
If you arrive alone—it is lonely
If you brought others with you
It is a celebration

~~Have a Nice Day~~
Make it a Great Day

It might not start right at the beginning
Maybe not
Oh! But it is there
The possibility— the pulling force
Ask yourself— Why are you resisting?
Let yourself meander
Release the constrictions
Remove the distractions
Close your eyes— paint a picture in your mind
Travel unrestricted
The smile you feel— lets you know you have arrived
Realize the lightness of your body
Your mind and your being
This feeling is free

You have made it a great day

Walk Beside Me

My hope is to inspire but not to be your inspiration
Let me bring freshness
Let me bring smiles
Let me be a voice to cast out thoughts
Let me be a listening ear to hear
Let me be a non-judgmental being for your inner self
Let me add lightness to your steps

No!

Do not make me your inspiration—
    that requires you to walk behind me to follow
I need you instead to walk beside me as a friend—
    that way when we need support we can reach out and
    walk hand-in-hand

If you are not going to do anything
Until you do it well— you are right
You are not going to do anything

What Am I Taking with Me?

Unbelievable stimulation
Brought about by accumulation
Enriched through investigation
Enhance with admiration
Molded according to inspiration
Enjoyed during observation
Forever imprinted within my sensations

What am I taking with me?
Numerous thoughts crossing my mind
Closed eyes of unending visions
Nostrils recalling lingering aromas
Lips that froze in a smile from reminiscing'
A back that has gladly shared the weight
Willing hands that reached out— lifted up— folded in thanks
Ears that have heard the echoing sounds
A soul filled with treasures put there by many
A heart that has loved what it is leaving behind
The footsteps that walked me through my time

I Wonder

Where the breeze starts or stops
Where the waves begin or end
I wonder
What I have done
For you to be my friend
I wonder
What tomorrow will bring— if I will complain and whine
Appreciation would come from those
Who have run out of time
I wonder
If the frogs croak when I am not there
Will the flowers bloom without my care

I wonder no more for now I have learned
Life is not about me— but rather my living through
The appreciation of you

Remain Open

Just a day
Nothing stirring
Not contemplating moving
Then I feel a gentle breeze
It comes— it goes— it comes again
Only this time it stirs more than the trees
Refreshing energy swirls my mind
Maybe I should move— explore— wander
I begin to think of destinations
Places I have not been taking time to go
What is calling me there…
Who is calling me there…
Where is this place…
Have I been there before…
How will I arrive…
Today I choose to go with the wind

No matter how you slice it
Bread is bread

Connect

If I were a wave, I would rush to the shore
I would cover your feet
Splash your body
And together we would smile
My approach starts when I see you coming to the shore
I would rise up
Curl like the "a" in "anticipate"
Put my crest down
Charge like a bull
Knock you over
And together we would laugh
I never tire
I back off, recharge
Find you again and again
If I were a wave
I would search for something to carry with me
I would bring it to you
You would be aware
Carry it home to become your treasure
I would always be your memory of
The day you and nature made a nice connection

Welcome Back

YES!
I see you coming to the shore
I have been coming and going searching
For the laughter we shared a time before
When I rose up— curled like the "a" in "anticipate"
Put my crest down— charged like a bull—knocked you over
And together we did laugh
Today you walk along my shoreline
You contemplate— every drop of me listens
So close— sometimes erasing your footprints left behind
Feeling my pull on the sand under your feet
You inch sideways to be closer to the dry beach
But I know to get you to lighten up and laugh is my feat
AAH!
A treasure I will bring for you to keep
Bring it close— but just out of reach
You move in on the keepsake—losing your focus on me
I charge like a bull— I set myself free
A forceful crash— a nature's bath
Another nice connection that made us laugh

Anticipate

Not always
    Maybe always
        Sometimes always
            Never quite sure
                But it seems to me
If you have made contact with something once
It is never to be experienced in a fresh way again
If all your focus is on anticipation
Anticipation is a precondition that tells you what it
    should be before you know what it is you anticipate
Release the old to the wind— while you anticipate an
    experience that has freshness
Anticipate— rediscover— take a different route— an
    approach not thought of before
Discover an awareness of something not noticed last time
Live anticipate— not anticipation
Fresh details will show up
In what you remember releasing to the wind

Hopeful

Hope without effort— a play without a director
Effort brings out being full of hope put forth with direction
Hopeful gives confidence a place to breed
Hopeful is the trait that waits for the opportunity to inspire
Hopeful keeps the eye watchful
The nose keen
The ear in tune to pick up the rhythm
The taste buds to savor the freshness
The desire to feel alive and the sensation of joy to celebrate the completeness of the task
The opportunity to learn from the experience you put forth
Keep hope full of effort— to inspire being optimistic

Why I hug a tree
I love anything with more wrinkles and crevices
than me

Bald Eagles

Watchers of the river
Roosting peacefully within the trees
A stately pose to conserve their energy
Glistening white feathers that are their crown
Two magnificent jewels embedded within
Give that look of integrity
The arched golden beak with its distinctive hook
Give the watchers of the river—their royal completed look
A determined lift from off their thrones
The spreading of wings like a royal robe
Talons are tucked under their brilliant white tails
The watchers of the river—are majestically in the air
Spontaneous movement of unbelievable grace
Soaring, gliding, spiraling, rising and focusing
Watching the river for their quest
Charging the river—as they ready their talons
Skimming the surface and then a quick snatch
Leaving as dignified as they arrive— to feed on their catch

Go With the Wind

Today I am the wind
I wait for you around the corner
I could twirl you around
    if you become too serious
I could carry laughter to your ears
    that can bring lightness to your feet
I could wrap myself around you
    and together dance the rhythm in a new step
I could be the gentle breeze
    that cools you down
I could be the source to blow away your stress
    as you celebrate between the gust your quest
I could wait for you with your kite
    together we would discover new heights
Come move through life with me today
Sometimes it refreshes oneself to go astray
Catch a new attitude— change the one you have got
You can or you cannot
Your choice means a lot

Air carries the heavy planes
Water carries the weight of a ship
And you complain—about carrying out the trash

Serene

A garden
Meandering paths
Mounds to add dimension
Rocks for a place to sit and contemplate
Hues that resemble an artist's pallet
Swirling clouds of whites that add fluff
Flowing lava in pigments of reds and orange
Yellows that glow to match the rising sun
Shades of blue reflecting the shadowy sky on water
   makes
Purples that blend with pinks to paint a sunset to walk in
Fragrant smells too rich to be contained in any bottle
Sounds of rustling in a gentle breeze
Linger— absorb the sense of tranquility

You might be the only one in the room
Who thinks they have hidden the elephant

Wind Rhythm

If the wind brings laughter
> follow it to find joy

If the wind brings the sounds of a symphony
> seek out the chair left empty for you

If the wind brings a melody of vibrations
> follow as you sing along

When the wind stirs around you
> take the lead and dance

If the wind is quiet
> let your joy start the vibrations

There are others waiting for their lead
> laughter is the *Ready, Set, Go* they need

Leave ostentatiousness to the peacocks

Courageous

Courage is an end product
       that is not alive
       an empty statement
       until someone has strived
To use courage as a description it cannot be
       nothing has happened to prove that thought
       courage hangs out— but there is nothing to see
       give courage life through actions you have
       brought
Now, courageous you are— I know for sure
I have witnessed your actions in many regards
       without whining you accept the challenge
       making the best out of the cards
Courageous is your feat you put on display
When you accept a challenge and with it you stay

◊◊◊

You wish for "Peace on Earth"
I wish you realize it starts
with cleaning your room

◊◊◊

Take Part

The difference created in a day
The opportunities are great to make it your way
The memories brought to the surface with flair
    might be your answered prayer
The thoughts that come to your mind may linger
Keep the best in focus and let the rest malinger
Smiles that continue to warm the heart
    your face I am sure is where they got their start
Thoughtfulness felt without a touch comes to your mind
    making memories never to be lost to time
Days are better if you bring something to the table
You will be more welcomed
    because you show you are able
    to make each day as interesting as a fable

Just Happens

Did not write it down
I thought I would remember
Well! I did not remember
    so I started writing it down
Oh! I wrote it down
    but cannot remember what I wrote it on
Now! I remember what I wrote it on
    cannot remember where I put it
What a mess on my refrigerator
    my keeping track has never been greater

This condition might go with me to a parking lot
I do not always remember the right spot
I know I drove my car to the store
Sometimes do not enter and exit the same door
So if you hear a beep—beep—beep—beep
    look towards the sound— smile and wave
It might be me
    using my special key

Watch the animals
They have a direct line to "Mother Nature"

Moved to My Heart

I lost a friend today
Not the lost you feel when you get separated at the mall
Not the lost you put on a milk carton
Not the lost by being misplaced
No! This is a loss of creating more memories
This loss brings about the change
From knowing to wondering
I take you with me in my heart— we will continue to
    count the Queens in the meadows
    watch the sun rise and set
    marvel at the rainbows
    explore the unbeaten paths
    take the time to find and smell the roses
    find a bench by the water big enough for two
I will sit and next to me I will sense you
You are in my heart and I am under your wings
Having appreciated life— peace it does bring

Wake Up Call

Realize life is around you
Not about you

The "Yesterdays" are gone
The "What if's" may never show
It is "Now" that has arrived

Feel the rhythm— dance the dance
See the beauty—enjoy the feast
Hear the movement— lighten your load
Taste the possibilities— savor the differences
Smell the opportunities—inhale deeper

You have heard before
But is your present listening
Awake to the freshness
Open your eyes
Let your imagination flow
Listen to your own heart
And know

This wakeup call is for you

Aaaaah! The Bench

Aaaaah!
A place to relax, to wonder, to remember
Aaaaah!
A place from which to observe, not judge
Aaaaah!
A place to renew thoughts and appreciate being
I could be waiting for you at the water's edge
Aaaaah!
We could sit together and replenish
We would absorb the moisture
You for the dried out memories
Me for the dried out cells
You would talk, I would listen
      and together we would put laughter
      and wisdom into the air
If you came upon me in a downtown area
I would be waiting for moments in time
When we sit and wonder
      where the rest of the world thinks they are going
      and why they are moving at such a fast pace
Our thoughts are the same—
Hope they find a bench when they get there
Take the time to sit, relax, and appreciate being

I have enjoyed this quiet time together
        as you continue your journey through life
I will or a relative of mine will be waiting
Your presence is rewarding
We love to give support

As the river flows
so does time

There But Not There

I got lost in my chair
Oh! It has happened before
It is not a scary feeling
It is not an empty feeling
No, it is a peaceful feeling
The feeling of being there but not there
I do not know if I get lost at first
Or if it is when I am approaching the
middle
I have learned not to worry
It seems to happen differently with
different things
I know when I finish
And close it shut
That finding a good book and being able
to read
Makes me appreciate my good luck

Gazing Ball

Your circle of life reflected here
Continues to be what you visualize in this sphere
It is your circle— it is what you believe
Only you should decide who enters or leaves
Physical things have a tendency to disappear
The memories left behind— become so dear
Take a stroll to where you find a sphere
Sense laughter— loving energy as you draw near
A cup of coffee in hand
Sit—kneel—or stand
Appreciate the precious present
Surrounding love is your accompaniment
Memories come alive to fill the void
That keep the circle intact
Be open so you feel the love
That is reflected right back

Still yourself
It is not always your job to talk

Birth of the Garage Sale

It starts with a little piece of this
        and a lot of that
Shoved in places
        do not remember for sure where it's at

Shoved in places
        so no one can see
        collection of stacks of this and that
They are starting to haunt me

A push to the side
        a slide to the back
        makes a little more room
        for some more this and that

Doors if I open
        may not close
        my little piece of this and my lot of that
        like a mountain grows

Do I need more of this
Do I need more of that
Another piece of furniture with virgin space

The time has arrived for me to unpack

No receipts can be found
        for my little piece of this and my lot of that
        my once thought treasures are waiting for you
Welcome to my garage sale out back

My Shadow

If together we are the end
The finale
The fat ladies that get to sing
Would we have known it...
Could we have felt it...
Should we have heard it...
We would not worry
For we have lived our way to it
Prepared for it
And always ready yesterday
Together we have realized
The end of one thing— a new beginning
Thanks for singing with me

The cost is one dollar
You have ninety-nine cents
The penny you could not be bothered to pick up
Takes on a whole new meaning

Rethink

It is what it is
Some would like to believe
Is an expression for a matter- of-fact approach to life
Give it some thought it just cannot be
It is what it is
An acceptance of stagnation
An inspiration that is going nowhere
Most of the same with nothing to expect
Imagination that no longer is there
Glad Edison did not believe
Or in the dark from sunset to sunrise we would still be
GW Carver must not have thought it okay
Or life would be without his P.B. and J.
Saying it is what it is— is really thinking backwards
Put it to rest as you repeat
It was what it was
It no longer applies
On this the first day of the rest of your life

What Are You Doing Today?

If I were a sailboat, I would beg to go to the sea
Love to feel the water splashing on my old dry boards
Hum as the wind blows across my bow
Rock up and down with the rhythm of the waves
Tug at the rope that is holding me back
Set myself free to go with the wind
Make no promise of return
I would think of you often with feet on dry ground
I would like it a lot if on my deck you were found
COME SAIL WITH ME

Just because you can
Does that mean you should?

The true strength of a tree
Is in its ability to bend

Something Inside

I am the something that lives in your
pocket
I might be still
I might be quiet
But I would be ready
I would burst out when you need laughter
I would whisper to encourage
From your pocket I would tame the
Butterflies in your stomach
Sometimes suggest a time-out
Intercept the words that try to
Escape before we have counted to ten
I live in your pocket so I can flex my
muscles
When you need strength
I help you to dream and think why not
I like being close to you
And when you reach in and give me that
hug.
I like your touch
I am glad I fit all pockets.

Do not just feel the breeze
Use all your sense to absorb the treasure

The Future's Pioneer

Why are you here?
None of this you own
For those yet to come you are their pioneer

Protect the frontier
Beware of the tone
For those yet to come you are their pioneer

Keep their future treasure near
Nurture the seeds you have sown
For those yet to come you are their pioneer

When your time ends you shed no tears
The pattern now you have grown
For those yet to come you are their pioneer

Appreciation from a future tenant that will be here
Leave no footprints in the established zone
Why are you here?
For those yet to come you are their pioneer

If it takes someone else to do more than
enhance your happiness—
You do not have all the ingredients for the recipe

A Walk in the Forest

Walk in the forest
Journey through stages in time
Nature's gems
Waiting for you to find

Invisible energy
Fills the air at all levels
Be open to absorption
Continue the journey using your senses

Notice the trees that have more wrinkles than you
Movement to Nature's unfinished symphony
Places to sit-stand or kneel
Filtered sun-reflected light-patches of shade for your
   delight
Rustling leaves-a whistling breeze-fallen trees
Come to rest on the forest floor

Scurrying tenants we hear but do not see
Birds singing as you continue your walk some more
Smoothness of new growth

Freshness of a breeze
Many textures are here
Use your sense of touch wisely please

Smells that resemble those from an attic
A whiff of freshness after a rain
Odor of things moving above and below the ground
Rich aromas from everything trigger the brain

Nature's table in a forest is always prepared
Food chains in action-the circle of life on display
Meats-nuts-roots-berries-leaves-branches- await
Educate yourself before you partake
So this is not your doomsday

Whatever

Whatever is never an answer
Whatever is never a final thought
Whatever tells your listener
It could be a commitment you have brought
Whatever is an idea— an open possibility
    subconsciously— whatever translates
Whatever needs to be done— I could pull my weight
Whatever I could do for you— I could do it
Whatever my load is— I could carry it
Whatever you are saying it is now in my subconscious
As a resource to rethink my thoughts
Whatever is open-ended and carried in the breeze
And now where it goes we will just wait and see

But duuuuuh! Dies silently right after it leaves

Move to the Slow Lane

You think it might have been today
        not sure
Everything goes so fast
It is like a blur
Maybe not today or yesterday
        or the day before that
Maybe tomorrow
        or the day after that
Maybe you have missed it
Maybe it is yet to come
Remember all days are precious
Spend them with gratitude
You may not have tomorrow
If you have a tomorrow
You will have the gratitude of memories of yesterday
To appreciate the slow lane today
The joy in enjoy is yours to share

Potential Snow People

Imagine being millions of years old and still dependable
Age and years of practice create a timetable of their own
Potential snow people are full of surprises
Either by arriving early and catching everyone off guard
Or those years when they arrive later than usual
Just when you begin to believe they are not going to
   show up
THEY ARRIVE!
Potential snow people have a variety of styles for their
   arrivals
Arrivals that are soft and slow suggest a waltz
Their potential parts glide to the ground
Resting like fresh slipcovers to hide what is underneath
I have seen want-to-be snow people in such a hurry to
   reach the ground
I wonder if I am wearing the wrong pair of glasses
When potential snow people hook up with the wind
They have a 747 type landing that overshoots the
   runway and piles up somewhere
After they arrive they have been known to lie around and
   sleep for months

Some of these potential snow people have become
   outstanding in society
One thing these potential snow people have in common is
   excitement when the sun shines
Their parts seem to awaken through vibrations and then
   they just run off
Oh yes! They will return next year— but live in the
   precious present
Take the opportunity to touch something, to throw
   something, or make an angel out of something that is
   millions of years old

Do it now before they run off

◊◊◊

Your birth certificate is your dance card for life
Carry your own punch

◊◊◊

About Ann

Ann was raised on a poultry farm east of Allegan, Michigan and graduated from Allegan Public Schools and Western Michigan University. She returned to Allegan, married Jim Chestnut, and raised two children on a dairy farm south of Allegan, where she still lives.

Teaching for Allegan Public Schools, rock collecting, helping others, and channeling her imagination through the arts is her daily motivation. Her poetry is achieved through appreciating and staying in touch with Mother Nature and her inhabitants.

In Ann's words, "I enjoy listening to people directly—at other times to words carried on the wind. Poetry comes to me through the body language of others. Not better-not worse-than mine, just different.

"Poetry can come to me as interrupted rain showers, a gentle continuous rain, or a thunderstorm that keeps my attention until it's done."

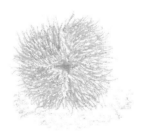

Made in the USA
Middletown, DE
23 May 2015